HOW I BECAME GOOD IN THE ROOM

By

Angelo Bell

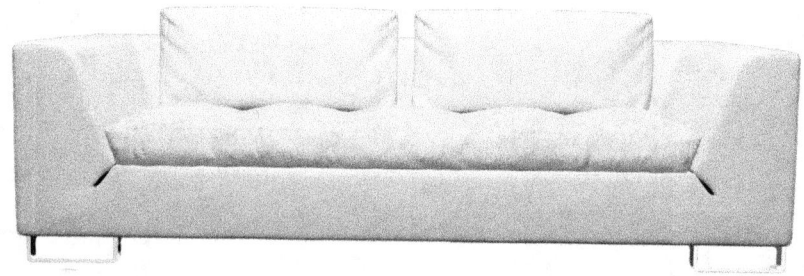

© Genepunk Publishing 2024

How I Became Good in the Room

From Screenwriter to TV Pilot Producer:
Building Credentials that Open Doors

Table of Contents

INTRODUCTION
TRUTH ABOUT BEING GOOD IN THE ROOM
UNDERSTANDING THE TV INDUSTRY
DEVELOPING YOUR SKILLS AND KNOWLEDGE
    Spreading the Word
    Hillcrest High School English Teacher
WHAT DOES IT MEAN TO BE GOOD IN THE ROOM?
GETTING IN THE ROOM
    The Robert Rodriguez Affect
UNDERSTANDING THE PITCH PROCESS
PITCHING TO NETWORK TV EXECUTIVE
NAVIGATING REJECTION AND FEEDBACK
CASE STUDIES AND SUCCESS STORIES
    Case Study #1
    Case Study #2
    Case Study #3
    Case Study # 4
CONCLUSION
ALL PITCHES
APPENDIX
    Glossary of Industry Terms

INTRODUCTION

Hello everyone, my name is Angelo Bell, and this is the story of how I mastered being "good in the room." But what does that actually mean? In Hollywood, it refers to sitting in front of powerful, wealthy, and influential studio executives, maintaining their interest with a commanding presence as you pitch a movie or television series idea. Being "good in the room" involves charisma, understanding what your audience wants, and a mix of other variables. For me, it often came down to personality and drawing from experiences that had nothing to do with Hollywood, filmmaking, or television production, but were still incredibly useful in this environment.

Interestingly, the title "How I Became Good in the Room" is a bit of a misnomer. It implies that I always aimed to be good in the room, which couldn't be further from the truth. I mention this so you understand that, no matter how far you feel from achieving this skill, you can become exceptional at it. It takes time, practice, and a few other elements, none of which are insurmountable. If I could do it, you can too.

The filmmaking and television industry have evolved significantly since I started. During the short period I was making films independently, the changes were dramatic and mind-boggling. I began at a time when film was the only option—you either used 8 mm or 35 mm, and that was it. This came with development costs, medium handling costs, and many other expenses. Today, you can grab your iPhone and make a movie. The transformation has been remarkable.

In my day, big movie stars would never dream of appearing in a television commercial. Nowadays, top-tier blockbuster film stars do commercials like it's just another day at DreamWorks Studios. Back then, these movie stars would only film commercials internationally, so their faces would appear on billboards in Japan, South Korea, China, and other places, but never in the United States. There was a stigma attached to being a big movie star and shooting commercials for American television.

The television industry itself has changed drastically. We have no abundance of television channels and networks available for everyone to see. I won't delve into how that came about—that's for another book—but with the rise of cable, digital networks, independent networks, and streaming services, there are countless venues where you can work as a producer.

Whether you work for Netflix, Tubi, Pluto, or another network that may or may not collaborate with independent film producers, the opportunities are exponentially greater than whenI started making films in 2002. It's amazing to see young men and women on YouTube now, with their side hustles as content creators, talking about making six figures on Tubi by shooting a $10,000 independent film.

I remember when my goal was to walk into a big studio like Warner Brothers or a major corporation like Netflix and pitch a new film or television series, or try to sell them an independent movie I made for less than $10,000. The process was intimidating, but now, it's probably the easiest it has ever been to step into someone's office and pitch your project.

If you're like me, you understand that hindsight is 20/20. Knowing what I know now, my life would have been different, and I hope this book equips you with the understanding that there is a way to succeed. It just takes a bit of effort.

To wrap up this introduction, I want to emphasize that it has never been easier to stand out from the crowd. Many people are so caught up in their feelings, in notions of fair play and justice, and in overinflated evaluations of their self-worth that they aren't willing to put in the extra effort to get the job done. To stand out, all you need to do is add an extra 10 to 15% to your efforts. If you want to move leaps and bounds ahead of the crowd, give an extra 30 to 40%. Work a little harder, work at night, and work without expecting immediate financial compensation. This effort is for you.

Now is the easiest time to step up, stand out from the crowd, and be recognized for the value you can bring to a studio, streaming service, or network television affiliate. All you have to do is get out there and do the work.

TRUTH ABOUT BEING GOOD IN THE ROOM

First, I'm going to share something with you that no one knows—I haven't told this to a soul. As you read on, you'll understand what I'm referencing.

From 2011 to 2015, I pitched projects to a major television network. But that's not my secret. My secret is that I was so terrified of walking into an office and pitching my idea for a television series to a studio executive that, for the first year, I never asked for an in-person pitch meeting. Instead, I submitted over 20 television series pitches in written format because I was too scared to pitch in person. As an introvert, the idea of selling myself was very uncomfortable.

At the beginning of the second year, the organization I was a part of had a second producer's meeting. During that meeting, I learned that nearly fifty percent of the producers in the room had gone on an in-person pitch meeting. I was the one the few who hadn't. These producers were talking to the studio executives as if they were all chums.

As I sat in that room of about 300 independent producers, I realized I was on the verge of complete and total failure. I was confident that, as a writer, I was as good as anyone in that meeting. Yet, they had achieved something I hadn't.

I made a decision at that moment: from now on, I would request an in-person pitch meeting every single time. My goal became to secure my first pitch meeting. About three months later I nabbed my first pitch meeting for a sci-fi based dramedy.

By the end of the three years, my production company and maybe 10 or 20 other companies were the only ones still standing, still pitching, and still reaching for success.

By the end of those four years, my production company had made a name for itself for being creative, dynamic, persistent, and enjoyable to work with. We secured six-figure deals to work on developing pilot scripts for two TV networks.

UNDERSTANDING THE TV INDUSTRY

The structure of the television industry is quite simple. While there are many books, YouTube videos, and other resources that offer a more in-depth understanding, I'll give you a basic overview. The television industry consists of networks, studios, and production companies. Production companies collaborate with producers, actors, and other creative talents to develop projects. To finance these projects, they often partner with studios. Networks then use their global resources to distribute these projects to audiences worldwide through various mediums and charge advertisers for airtime. In essence, the industry revolves around making money by creating content that attracts viewers, so your job as a producer is to balance artistic or entertaining content with marketability.

Within the television industry, there are several types of services: network television (regular TV), cable television (subscription-based service), and streaming services (subscription-based but not available through normal broadcasts). Despite their differences, they all aim to provide high-quality content that draws audiences to their platform, allowing them to charge more for subscriptions. Nowadays, even services like Netflix and Hulu, which were previously ad-free, have incorporated ads, making advertising a central aspect once again.

Remember that ad buyers only want to be associated with certain types of projects, so keep this in mind when writing and creating your content.

Additionally, there are platforms like YouTube and other digital content creation forums that independent filmmakers can leverage. These platforms have lower requirements and barriers to entry, making them accessible alternatives for content distribution.

DEVELOPING YOUR SKILLS AND KNOWLEDGE

Let's discuss developing your skills and knowledge to become confident and effective in meetings with studio executives. Several pathways can guide you toward becoming a well-spoken, commanding presence in the room. Many factors influence your ability to succeed, and it's up to you to be aware of these factors, using them when necessary or discarding them if they have adverse effects. Assess your strengths and weaknesses in speaking and human interaction, and identify ways to navigate around your shortcomings. Take stock of your abilities, flaws, and assets.

For me, it was always about personality. As a young man, I was very shy and introverted. I was quiet in school and around strangers, known as the "Quiet One." But deep inside, I yearned to be outgoing, confident, and charming—the kind of person who could talk to anyone, make people laugh, and effortlessly converse with girls. To achieve that, I read countless books and magazine articles from Esquire, Cosmopolitan, and others on topics like mastering small talk, being the life of the party, and becoming the person everyone turns to. From age 10 to 18, I devoured more than a thousand articles because I didn't want to remain introverted. Each article helped me, along with a few books.

Other experiences also shaped me. For example, I did an internship at a hospital in Queens, New York, through a pre-med endorsement program in high school. That summer, I came into contact with a patient with tuberculosis. There were seven or eight of us from school working as interns to qualify for the pre-med endorsement on our diplomas, but I was the only one who tested positive for tuberculosis exposure because I had fed a patient who should have been quarantined. I had to take medicine for a year, and to this day, if I take a DPT test, it always shows up positive, so I need a chest X-ray instead.

During that hospital internship, I cleaned up, emptied bedpans, fed patients, and dealt with a cranky old man who hated young Black boys. Despite the challenges, two girls worked there, and while I had a crush on one, the other was more friendly toward me. I remember the anxiety I felt in the elevator, struggling to say something to impress the girl I liked. Ultimately, I ended up looking like a geeky dork who didn't know how to talk to women and was friend-zoned. However, this experience played a vital role in shaping who I became as an adult. By the end of that summer internship, I resolved never to let that happen to me again.

Spreading the Word

During my first marriage, my wife was a preacher's kid (PK); her father was a pastor at a local church. Consequently, she grew up in the church, and we attended regularly. When we had children, we also took them to church. As time went on, I became increasingly involved in church activities. With a strong work ethic, I always volunteered to help whenever something needed to be done.

As a result, I eventually became a deacon, then the lead deacon, and finally the chairman of the board of deacons. This progression caused some issues because other young men who had been in the church longer than I had resented my rapid advancement. However, as I mentioned earlier, it's not difficult to stand out if you're willing to do what others are not.

My experiences in church significantly influenced how I interacted with studio executives during meetings. Frequently, I had to stand up in front of our congregation, and sometimes in front of visiting congregations during events like the pastor's anniversary or the church anniversary. I had to engage the audience, encourage them to participate, and create an atmosphere of praise and celebration.

These experiences of speaking and leading in church helped me immensely when I found myself in a room with executives, pitching my ideas for TV series. The confidence and public speaking skills I developed were invaluable in those high-pressure situations.

Hillcrest High School English Teacher

Another significant influence was my high school teacher, Ms. Sullivan. She was a short, feisty woman in her sixties, as mean as a snake but for some reason, she liked me. Ms. Sullivan was adamant about helping students understand the difference between how they spoke and how they wrote.

I had already decided long ago that I wanted to be a writer, so her advice was crucial to me. She said, "You should speak like you write." To me, this meant that slang, colloquialisms, and street vernacular had no place in structured writing, and therefore, they shouldn't be part of verbal communication either.

I made a point of speaking as I wrote. As a young man, I was often teased by friends and classmates for "speaking like a white boy" or speaking "too perfectly." They meant that I wasn't using the same slang they did; I preferred to use proper words. This preference led me to learn new words regularly and remember the adage that if you use a word three times correctly in a sentence, it becomes yours.

This approach greatly affected my interactions with studio executives. Speaking clearly and effectively played a significant role in my success, and I was always aware of that, using it to my advantage.

WHAT DOES IT MEAN TO BE GOOD IN THE ROOM?

Let's take a moment to delve into what it really means to be "good in the room." Does it mean being charismatic? Probably. Does it mean knowing how to inspire a crowd? Most likely. But does it mean you always get the sale? Absolutely not.

Being good in the room means giving 100% of your best effort when you step into that executive's office. It means doing your homework, knowing your plan, having a solid strategy, and being well-rehearsed. It also means considering different possibilities and being ready to pivot at a moment's notice when faced with resistance.

Being good in the room isn't about your win-to-loss ratio. It's about making a lasting impression with your concept, professionalism, and creativity.

One thing being good in the room doesn't mean is being unmoved by the stress of the situation. Walking into a studio executive's office could mean there are hundreds of thousands, if not millions, of dollars on the table to be won or lost. It's like a high-stakes game of poker or blackjack. You might maintain a calm exterior, but inside, it's turmoil and chaos.

Despite my many pitch meetings, I always get nervous. I'm always worried I'll say or do something wrong or completely foolish. I'm always worried I'll freeze. I'm always worried the person sitting opposite me will dislike me for reasons beyond my control. I'm always worried I'll appear too aggressive or too soft, too flighty or too stubborn, too open or too narrow-minded.

When I realized I was still getting nervous after my 10th pitch meeting, I decided to let the nervousness in. I got this trick from the pilot episode of "Lost." There's a scene where the main character, Jack, talks about nearly paralyzing a young girl during an operation when he made a mistake. He describes how fear threatened to overwhelm him.

Jack decided to let the fear take over completely for five seconds. He didn't resist or try to stifle it. He gave the fear five seconds to do its worst, and then he moved on.

I also learned from an Esquire magazine article that people who fear public speaking should admit their fear to the audience. Once they admit it, they no longer have to hide it. This honesty puts both the speaker and the audience on the same page, and at ease, thereby reducing much of the stress and anxiety.

So, before any meeting with executives—whether it was for alternative programming, reality shows, soap operas, sitcoms, dramas, or procedurals—I would take a seat in the lobby and say to myself, "Angelo, you're nervous about this meeting, and it's okay to be nervous." If someone was with me, I'd tell them, "It's okay to be nervous because I'm nervous too."

If I still felt paralyzed by fear and nervousness when I walked into the office, I would tell the executive, "Can you give me a moment? I'm a little nervous right now." More often, I refused to start my pitch until I got the basic pleasantries out of the way and calmed down. I'd talk about the weather, traffic, weekend plans, a show on their network, or even the pineapple hanging in one executive's office that was part of a hit show.

I viewed it as my meeting and my time. If I needed a couple of minutes to chill, I took them. And I'm happy to say that I never messed up. I never offended anyone or put my foot in my mouth. I can't say the same for some of the folks who came with me, but I always kept my cool. My production company became the most talked-about company for the parent network because we succeeded more often than not.

GETTING IN THE ROOM

Getting into the room is as mysterious as David Blaine's best trick. It's like when people see something amazing and wonder, "How the heck did he do that? How in God's name did he make that happen?" I remember when I was starting out in filmmaking, the idea of pitching terrified me. I'd hear stories or read articles about someone unexpectedly meeting a famous director on a studio lot, handing over their screenplay, and making history in a single meeting. And like everyone else, I'd think, "How did they even get onto that studio lot at Warner Bros in the first place? That's the real secret everyone wants to know."

So, how do you get in the room? When I first started writing, my goal wasn't to get into the room. I just wanted to write—I dreamed of being a Hollywood screenwriter, crafting blockbuster movies that grossed $100 million and afforded me a mansion in the Hollywood Hills or Pacific Palisades. I wanted nothing to do with the hustle of selling my screenplay; I imagined my agent handling all of that while I focused on writing and collecting the checks.

The Robert Rodriguez Affect

But around 2001-2002, figures like Quentin Tarantino, Robert Rodriguez, and others emerged who were making waves with their independent projects. I was writing feverishly, sending my scripts to agents and companies, but no one was biting. Caught up in the indie filmmaker wave, I decided to take matters into my own hands and make my own films. The problem? My scripts were written for big Hollywood budgets—my passion and my dream.

Unable to afford these grand productions, I researched how these filmmakers got started. That's when I discovered the world of short films. Long story short, I decided to write and direct a short film. As I wrote, I immersed myself in learning every aspect of filmmaking—directing, filming, photography, editing—much like how Robert Rodriguez did with his debut film, "El Mariachi," where he was a one-man crew.

In 2002-2003, I embarked on creating my first short film. I had to learn everything—from organizing casting calls and auditions, to finding actors and evaluating their previous work. As a producer, editor, and cinematographer, I navigated the challenges of shooting on DVC tape, a format that required the entire tape to be digitized for editing in Adobe Premiere, which I learned through a training program. I handled sound design, music selection, and post-production to bring my vision to life.

Once the film was completed, I faced the challenge of finding a venue to screen it, a crucial step for the cast and crew eager to see their work on the big screen. Despite the stress, I was hooked. The first film, a 12 to 19-minute endeavor, led to more projects. I negotiated for better locations and found a reliable crew, even as I changed jobs and invested my bonuses into weekend shoots.

Teaming up with a business partner, we founded a film production company and expanded our repertoire to include more short films and eventually a feature-length production. I delved into guerrilla filmmaking—making the most of limited resources, securing locations creatively, and maximizing production values.

As I remained immersed in the world of independent filmmaking, my efforts gained attention. With a growing following on Twitter, I produced six short films in 2006 alone, each showcasing my production company's name. Four of these films earned spots in the prestigious LA Shorts Film Festival, marking a significant milestone in my career.

During this period, crowdfunding platforms like Kickstarter and Indiegogo emerged as game-changers for filmmakers seeking funding. As I juggled production schedules, I also focused on legitimizing my production company by listing our films on IMDb. Mastering the intricacies of IMDb listings, I became a go-to resource for fellow filmmakers seeking guidance on navigating the platform.

By the end of this whirlwind journey, referencing my production credits on IMDb became a testament to my dedication and achievements in the film industry.

While I wasn't making money from my filmmaking experiences, I leveraged them when other producers sought my advice or guidance. Instead of financial compensation, I accepted film credits, which quickly multiplied my IMDb presence from four to six, then to eight, and eventually over ten credits. Some of these credits came from contributing financially to crowdfunding campaigns or earning executive producer titles.

Craigslist played a significant role in my journey. I regularly checked the "gigs" section for film production opportunities, volunteering my time in exchange for production credits. This grassroots approach helped build my portfolio and expand my network.

I maintained a blog where I openly shared my experiences and knowledge gained from volunteering with Film Independent. Frustrated by the secrecy surrounding filmmaking processes, I made it a point to demystify and share insights on digital video filmmaking. This not only boosted my personal visibility but also promoted my production company's name in the industry.

During this period, Blockbuster Video provided a unique avenue for filmmakers to gain exposure and revenue by distributing low-budget films. I pursued this route with two feature-length films, submitting them for direct-to-video distribution. Through this process, I connected with a Blockbuster reviewer tasked with evaluating submissions. Our professional rapport grew into a friendship, solidified when we coincidentally met at a film festival screening one of my shorts from the 24-hour film project.

Even after he moved to another studio, we stayed in touch. When I mentioned my independently produced genre films, he took them to the American Film Market with his new company, seeking a distribution opportunity.

At the American Film Market, held at the Santa Monica Loews Hotel, every room transforms into a screening venue where filmmakers from across the globe gather to sell their films. It was my first experience delving into the art of pitching, and I must admit, I was quite terrible at it. When my friend asked me to pitch my film idea in his suite, I stumbled over my words, stuttering and forgetting my lines. It was embarrassing and frustrating, to say the least.

His coworkers even came out from the back room to check on me, that's how bad it was. He told me then and there, "You've got to get good at this."

The goal was simple: navigate the hotel, meet with distributors, and pitch my film. Despite my initial ineptitude, I held onto a glimmer of confidence that with practice, I would improve. Perhaps not close a deal right away, but at least I'd stop sounding like a bumbling fool with each passing day.

Luckily, I was accompanying a talented filmmaker named Karina, who was pitching a Neo-Noir action film featuring an all-female cast. What I quickly learned was the power of her presence—distributors were eager to entertain her impromptu visits. I tagged along as she effortlessly secured meetings, and during these sessions, I refined my pitch by observing reactions and incorporating feedback from each distributor we met.

By day's end, my elevator pitch had been honed to perfection through repeated practice and adaptation. While we didn't secure a sale, we did walk away with contact information from several prominent distributors based in the USA, the Netherlands, and Canada.

I later documented my experience at the American Film Market in a three-part blog series that garnered thousands of views from fellow filmmakers. It solidified my company's reputation as a dedicated independent production house actively working to make significant strides in the industry.

UNDERSTANDING THE PITCH PROCESS

One of the key insights I gained from the American Film Market was understanding what executives look for—a crucial element of a successful pitch.

You can't approach a production company known for children's movies and pitch them a horror film or a genre film. Before you walk in, you need to do your research. Find out what projects they're currently developing and investing in. Understand their recent successes. Knowing who their audience is and what type of content they typically support takes away a lot of the pressure of convincing them that your project is the right fit.

Additionally, it's; that'so understand the type of talent they usually work with. If a production company typically casts B or C-list male leads, pitching them an idea centered on A-list stars like in "Charlie's Angels" would be a waste of time and could signal your lack of understanding of their preferences. Similarly, if they support brands aligned with women's empowerment, proposing a film that contradicts their values could alienate them.

For instance, pitching a scintillating young adult romance to Disney would not be wise—it wouldn't align with their brand.

Your pitch needs to include a compelling concept, unique selling points, and hooks that make it stand out. It must be original and demonstrate market viability. Written components like the logline, synopsis, and character breakdowns for lead roles are essential. Visual aids can be helpful but shouldn't overwhelm—bringing a few key images or a trailer that captures the essence of your vision can be effective.

Each of these elements plays a crucial role in crafting a persuasive pitch.

PITCHING TO NETWORK TV EXECUTIVE

So, how does one go about setting up a pitch meeting at a television network or streaming service like Netflix, Hulu, or others? How is it done?

The key is to establish an authentic, verifiable production company with credits. Personally, as a writer, I ventured into directing and producing my own films. I worked diligently to get those films listed on IMDb. Additionally, I supported my colleagues in making independent films, which earned me producer or executive producer credits on those projects.

But what if you're not a writer, director, or producer yet aspire to enter this arena? There are two paths you can take. First, invest time into creating films that bear your production company's name and get them listed on platforms like IMDb. Second, if you have the financial means, support aspiring filmmakers by financing their projects in exchange for a producer credit. You can also step in as a hands-on producer, connecting filmmakers with necessary resources throughout various stages of production, from pre-production to post-production.

In my case, it involved a combination of time and money. The crucial point is, you cannot approach major studios like Netflix, NBC Universal, Disney, or Columbia without a credible filmmaking or producing background. However, building this credibility is straightforward—you simply need to start.

Establishing your production company within the film industry not only provides immediate benefits but also sets the stage for future opportunities. A robust social media presence for your company, for instance, can yield unforeseen advantages. Despite initial uncertainties, your efforts will eventually pay off.

For me, having a strong social media presence and a substantial list of IMDb credits proved invaluable when I attended the American Film Market. It enabled my production company to secure a spot, which later led to a remarkable opportunity.

The American Film Market forged a partnership with the Independent Film & Television Alliance and NBC Universal and its affiliates. This collaboration allowed independent producers, including myself, to meet with NBCUniversal executives on their studio lot. While many of my peers had minimal IMDb credits and lacked established production companies, I had gone the extra mile. This effort placed me in a grand ballroom at Universal Studios alongside 500 other independent producers, receiving instructions on how to pitch ideas not only to NBC Universal but also to their extensive network of affiliates.

Having extensive meetings with numerous NBCUniversal executives provided me with the opportunity to forge a relationship with a production company in China. Doing business in China, Hong Kong, or other Asian countries is notoriously challenging for outsiders, as they typically prefer to work with familiar entities.

How did I overcome this barrier? During the American Film Market, a friend introduced me to a young woman from the Hong Kong Film Council. She graciously introduced me to several Hong Kong distributors and production companies. Once I shook hands with them, I transitioned from being a foreigner to someone they knew. Subsequently, they were responsive to my calls and emails, even sharing confidential insights into their filmmaking processes.

This introduction eventually led to an invitation to attend Filmart in Hong Kong a year later.

The additional effort, that extra 10%, often proves pivotal between achieving success or stagnation.

It's crucial to adopt a producer's mindset. When you enter that room, you're not merely a writer eager to see your story on screen—instead, you're a producer orchestrating a project that benefits everyone involved, including the studio or network executives. Approaching the pitch with a mindset of creating mutually beneficial outcomes is essential. If you enter solely focused on your story without regard for their time and needs, you risk losing their interest.

Conversely, if you approach the meeting thinking, presenting, and handling feedback like a seasoned professional, you increase your chances of progressing to the next stage.

More on that later.

NAVIGATING REJECTION AND FEEDBACK

So, what do you do when you're sitting in that room, passionately pitching your project and characters, only to have the person across from you shake their head and say, "This is not for us"? How do you stay motivated? Do you walk out?

Rejection is a significant part of this industry. You'll face it far more often than success. However, rejection and failure serve as directional arrows on the path to eventual success. The key is not to internalize rejection but to use it as a learning tool. Understand that while you fell short this time, it doesn't mean you'll always fall short.

Start by analyzing what went wrong. Did you overlook crucial research? Was there already a similar development? Did an actor attached to your project have a negative history with that studio? Perhaps you pitched a genre film to a drama-focused department.

You also need to determine if this rejection is an opportunity to pivot. Was there something in your pitch that turned the executive off? If you could go back, how would you approach it differently?

How can you refine and improve? These are the questions you need to address in real-time as you receive feedback and during your post-pitch evaluation.

I once attended a pitch meeting with the senior development executive of a network television studio's drama division. I was accompanied by a colleague—a young lady with whom I had previously pitched alternative and reality programming, but this was our first drama pitch together.

Our pitch felt strong to me, but within five minutes, it was clear this project wasn't resonating with him. I was ready to wrap up the meeting, but my colleague, more persistent than I, politely asked for clarification on why it wasn't a fit and explored the possibility of adjusting our project to align more closely with what he was seeking.

That initial "no" turned into a 30-minute casual conversation. We discussed the studio's direction, the executive's recent role at the studio, and strategies to better position our pitch for future meetings. Though we left without a yes, we gained a wealth of information—a gold mine that would inform our approach during the next pitch. I learned a valuable lesson that day.

CASE STUDIES AND SUCCESS STORIES

During my time pitching TV series ideas across various formats—alternative programming, reality, comedy, half-hour dramas, and sitcoms—I collaborated with several writers who brought creative concepts to the table. They would submit their ideas, we'd refine them together, and then I would guide them on adjustments based on the specific network affiliates I intended to pitch to, aligning with their programming preferences.

Many of these writers were new to the pitching process. By then, I had grown comfortable walking into those rooms, following a personal ritual to prepare myself for each pitch. My consistent advice to them was to remember that the goal of each meeting was simply to advance to the next one. It wasn't about closing a deal and walking out with a check. The pitch process unfolds in layers, and each step needs to be approached methodically and separately.

Case Study #1

I emphasized to each writer the importance of selling the series concept rather than getting lost in intricate character development and plot details during pitch meetings. It's crucial not to overwhelm executives with unnecessary information at this stage; the goal is to capture their interest in the series idea itself before diving into deeper elements like pilot episodes and character arcs.

One writer, in particular, had a compelling sci-fi concept tailored for a science fiction network. I guided him on identifying the core selling point of his idea—the societal implications—and advised him to streamline his pit around this key aspect. While he was passionate about exploring intricate plot nuances and character complexities, I stressed the need to prioritize clarity and brevity for a successful 20-minute pitch meeting.

During the pitch, I introduced the concept and set the stage, aiming to engage the executives. However, when it was his turn, he veered off-track into detailed plot points and character intricacies, losing the attention of our audience. Despite my attempts to steer back to the core hook of the series, he persisted in delving into his elaborate narrative elements.

As the executives' interest waned, and sensing the need to salvage the pitch, I intervened. Unfortunately, the persistence on his part to delve into intricate details led to a swift rejection. Reflecting on our experience afterward, I reminded him of the importance of sticking to the prepared pitch strategy we had discussed.

Outside the meeting, I candidly discussed the outcome with him. Despite our preparation and guidance, he expressed hesitancy about compromising his original vision during pitches. He acknowledged his fear of pitching and reluctance to alter his cherished idea, even if it meant missing out on a major network opportunity.

This experience underscored the common challenges in navigating the dynamics of pitching and the inherent human condition of holding onto creative control versus achieving broader success in the industry.

Case Study #2

Another incident involved collaborating with a production partner on a series idea that initially came to us through a third party pitch. While the concept showed promise, it needed refinement to align with what the network was seeking, based on my ongoing interactions with their executives over the past few years. Together, we reshaped the idea and successfully progressed to a second meeting with the executive team.

During this meeting, the executive provided extensive feedback, drawing comparisons to successful shows within their network's portfolio, such as a spy series known for its adherence to a specific format and thematic consistency. He emphasized the importance of maintaining the integrity and format of the genre throughout each episode.

I grasped the executive's point, but my colleague seemed to misunderstand. After the meeting, as we discussed over coffee in the courtyard, he interpreted the feedback as a directive to transform our idea into a spy show. I clarified that the executive was advising us to define and adhere to a clear format, not change genres.

Despite my explanation, my colleague persisted in wanting to pivot our concept towards espionage, even though we were already in the second meeting phase. It took considerable effort to convince him otherwise. At one point, I even suggested calling the executive for clarification, but cautioned that doing so could risk undermining our credibility if he had indeed misinterpreted the feedback.

Eventually, I persuaded him to abandon the idea of converting our drama into a spy series, emphasizing the importance of respecting the original concept and the executive's guidance on maintaining thematic consistency. This experience highlighted the challenge of interpreting and applying feedback correctly in pitching sessions, ensuring alignment with the network's expectations while preserving the integrity of our creative vision.

Case Study #3

I recall a memorable pitch session at a network affiliate with a friend of mine, our second or third meeting with them. Their office faced the afternoon sun, and the couch where I sat was directly in its path.

Being a larger guy, I naturally perspire, but the scorching Burbank heat amplified it. As I began my pitch with my usual enthusiasm and animated style, sweat started pouring down my forehead, dripping noticeably.

Mid-pitch, I couldn't help but think, "They must think I'm nervous as hell, sweating bullets." In reality, I was just uncomfortably hot. About two minutes in, I knew I had to address it. If I didn't stop, I'd be drenched by the five-minute mark. But where could I pause?

So, I did something unexpected. I halted, turned to the window where the sun blazed, turned back to them, and exclaimed, "Damn, it's hot in here!"

The executive immediately apologized and quickly fetched a napkin for me to dab my face. We shared a moment of levity as I joked about looking like I was sweating bullets. Despite not selling them on any of the pitches that day, I gained something invaluable: a rapport. I could now call ahead and ask, "Hey, I'm working on this idea about [blah blah blah], do you think it might interest you?" Their responses saved me time, whether they expressed interest or passed.

This experience underscored the power of honesty and human connection in business interactions. By turning a potentially awkward situation into a humorous and relatable moment, I strengthened our professional relationship and navigated future pitches with greater ease.

Case Study # 4

For four years, from 2011 to 2015, I diligently pitched to a major television network. In 2015, I finally achieved a breakthrough by selling TV series pilot scripts to the network. Although neither pilot script made it past the development phase, the financial rewards were substantial. One project secured a five-figure producer deal, while the second project earned a five-figure writer deal.

One deal was with a network affiliate that I held in high regard, presenting a serious opportunity to potentially see a show on their network. The other deal was with a network known for its alternative programming, exploring a shift into dramatic content. My colleague and I aimed to become the first African-American producers with a drama on their network.

I approached both opportunities with a long-term perspective. I believed in building a sustainable career rather than seeking quick paydays and fading away. Unfortunately, I observed many in the industry succumb to the allure of immediate financial gain, often at the expense of their long-term prospects. This disillusioned me with some of my business partners, whose actions eroded my optimism about a lasting career in TV and film.

Consequently, I took a step back for several years. Now, I've returned with renewed focus. The feedback on my most recent TV series pilot is promising, reigniting my determination to navigate the industry with resilience and integrity. Understanding the lessons learned from the people, challenges and from the experience, underscores my commitment to a sustainable career in television and film.

CONCLUSION

So, where does all this information lead you, and how can you, as a newcomer to the film and television industry, land your first pitch meeting with studio or network television executives?

The key takeaway from this book is that becoming effective at a pitch meeting doesn't demand special skills, training, or education akin to selling a luxury car to a wealthy buyer. Instead, you're meeting with people actively seeking projects to invest in—you just need to offer or develop what they want.

Crucially, you must possess credentials that instill confidence in your ability to deliver. Here's how you can achieve that:

Firstly, gain experience. Volunteer at film festivals, on film shoots, and sets. Immerse yourself in trade publications, online forums, and independent film groups. Find local filmmakers and offer your help, whether through time, money, or expertise, in exchange for credits as a producer.

Accumulate these credits on multiple films, ensuring each gets listed on IMDb. Promote these projects through blogs, social media, and other channels to establish your presence.

Within 6 to 9 months, aim to accumulate six to nine solid credits on your film production resume. Simultaneously, network with established industry groups, film councils, and professional organizations. Spread your name as a producer looking for projects, and connect with film funds and investors.

By 9 to 12 months, you should have a robust presence in the film community, attracting opportunities and projects to you. With these credentials and connections, you'll have the audacity to approach Netflix, Hulu, Disney, NBC, CBS, ABC, or other major networks for pitch meetings.

Remember, it only takes one successful pitch to open doors. If you have financial resources, you can expedite this process by investing in existing films as an associate producer or producer. This strategy can get your name on screens at numerous film festivals worldwide.

Credentials in this industry aren't about lengthy degrees; they're about action and experience condensed into achievable time frames. Anyone committed to becoming a producer and pitching network television shows can do so—it's a matter of taking initiative and leveraging your growing credentials effectively.

ALL PITCHES

Written and In-person

1. Tradecraft
2. Turbulence
3. Brutal Planet
4. Mummy Witch
5. Alien Theory
6. Apocalyptic Playground
7. White House Plague
8. Social Justice
9. Alternate
10. GP
11. Slightly Dead
12. Cannibals on the Underground Railroad
13. Dark Entity
14. Animus
15. Lab Rats
16. The Prince
17. Volcanoraptor
18. Angry Crows
19. Sinkhole Beach
20. Milk Badges
21. Legend of the Lotus
22. Wooden Nickel
23. Dust Devils
24. Interns
25. How to Save the World and Get the Girl
26. Realm
27. Bloody Bones
28. Mode
29. Channel 888
30. Mine-o-taur
31. Reckoning
32. King David
33. Ghost Ride
34. Sibling Factor
35. Carnival High
36. Cursed
37. Snowballs
38. Dread-Night
39. Family of the Year
40. Crime U
41. Backstab
42. Family Bond
43. Envy Me
44. All American
45. My Own Advice
46. Glam Wars
47. Bad Gnome
48. House of Adam
49. Ghost Valley
50. Glam Chat

51. Face Wars
52. Glam-It!
53. Offsides
54. Ex-Bride
55. Conspiracy
56. Dealing
57. Pop Life
58. North's of the Border
59. Guidance Counselor
60. Beer and Pizza
61. Lucaz
62. Night Beast
63. Psychic Stilettos
64. Preserved
65. Last Chance Dance
66. Exodus
67. Blackguard
68. Deep Harbor
69. Redemption
70. Deviant Behavior
71. Brand Gurus
72. Modern Men
73. Changes
74. Mummy's Curse
75. Blackfeather
76. An Accord
77. Family Tires
78. Paroled
79. Changes
80. Family Ties
81. Deviant Behavior
82. Sole-Men
83. Future City Challenge
84. The Best Clique
85. Good Medicine
86. Sister Factor
87. Adrift

APPENDIX

Glossary of Industry Terms

Producer
A producer does just that - produces things. When you're putting the project together, the producer produces the money, the crew, the equipment, etc. Anyone who has an essential part in making the project happen can be, and will probably want to be, called a producer.

Producers often package the film, raise money, oversee the budget, bring actors to the project, negotiate, and know the right people. They are variously known as executive, supervising, associate, co-, and line producers.

There are all sorts of names for producers: Executive Producer, Line Producer, etc. In my opinion, when you're doing a small independent production, it's senseless to bother with all the fancy titles. If you can have someone fill the job of Production Manager, that person will represent the producer(s) on set and make sure everything is running smoothly and according to budget. Most first-time producers will work independently, and some will also be the writer and director. It's tough, but someone can do it.

Director
The person responsible for translating the script onto film. He has overall responsibility for the artistic interpretation of the script. The director is the eye of the audience. A movie is a story told in moving pictures, and the director decides which pictures will best communicate the story to the audience. Directors

work closely with the other department heads (described below) and provide a unified vision of the finished project. The director also works with the actors, fine-tuning their performances so that they fit with the unified vision (left to their own devices, actors can be a pain in the arse.)

Directors have a lot of creative power over your production. A bad director can ruin a great script, and a great director can save a bad one. He or she is also responsible for the "feel" of the set. The screaming, frenetic directors we see characterized in movies would lead to a very uncomfortable set, a disgruntled crew, and probably a bad product. The director is the most essential member of the creative team. Choose him or her carefully.

Assistant Directors (ADs)
Usually, there are four: the first, second, third, and AD-in-training (TAD). I could go into lengthy descriptions of what each one does, but essentially, they all help the director communicate with the cast and crew to accomplish everything that needs to be done on schedule. You can get away with just a first, but he or she should have on-set experience. Without at least one AD, your director will go insane.

Big-budget productions hire a bunch of Production Assistants (PAs) as well. They do all sorts of things, from directing traffic to watching the parking lot, and work closely with the Locations Manager (LM). If you have enough money for PAs, you don't need to be reading this - just hire a producer who already knows what they're doing!

Director of Photography (DOP)
Also called cinematographers, DOPs are experts on the media you're shooting on (film, digital video, etc.) and the camera you're shooting with. Also known as

the D.P. or Cinematographer, creates (along with the director) the film's visual style. Responsible for what we will see and how we will see it (chooses film stock, recording medium, lenses, filters, camera placement and angles, etc.) Everything a movie cast and crew works for must pass through that little lens. They know how to light a scene to match the mood, set up the camera to match the director's vision, and make the thing look good. There's not much more I can say about it except that a good DOP is absolute gold. You know how some movies have breathtaking shots that make you feel like you're there, and some have crappy lighting and just look like sh*t? That's the difference between a good DOP and a bad one (also the quality of the post, but that's a whole other ball game).

Camera Operator
Well, what can I say? Camera Ops operate the camera. They should know the camera well and how to handle the media, along with all the camera equipment, such as dollies, steady-cam rigs, and camera cranes. They work under the direct supervision of the DOP and director and can save much time, money, and effort if they're good. It is very important to have an experienced camera op, but on really small productions, the DOP also operates the camera.

The Camera Operator can also have one to several assistants, depending on the budget, the media, and the camera equipment used. Film cameras often require a separate Focus Puller, for example, and dollies require someone to push them around. Work with the Camera Operator to figure out the requirements for your particular shoot. I recommend at least one camera assistant, though.

Sound Mixer and Boom Operator
Film cameras don't record sound directly onto the film, so a sound crew is essential. But even if you're

shooting on video, I suggest using separate sound recordings on your production. This provides for greater flexibility and higher-quality sound. Some will argue that it's not worth the hassle for a small indie production. In my opinion, they are lazy, and their product will sound terrible. Do it right the first time, blah, blah, blah.

Your Sound Mixer operates the mixing board where all the sound sources are recorded, and your Boom Op gets the microphones close to the actors without getting in the shot. A good sound crew will save you tons of headaches and make your final product much better. You can do everything else right, but if the sound sucks, so will your movie. These people are essential to the success of your project.

Gaffer, Grips, and Electrics
The Gaffer sets up the lights. It sounds simple, but it's a very complex job. The amount of hardware it takes to light a scene properly is astounding. If you don't have a lot of lights, then one person will suffice. If you want to light your project as the professionals do, plan on having an assistant for your Gaffer, or "Best Boy," a Key Electrics and assistants to supply the enormous amount of power needed for the lights, and a Key Grip and assistants to move everything around and set up the gear. Not to mention Transport to move the stuff from location to location. Even on small production, you'll do well to assign people to these key positions to make sure the gear you do have is handled properly and things get done on time. Most of the time it takes to make a movie is spent on lighting, so a good team in this area can make or break your shooting schedule.

Location Manager (LM)
Guess what - they manage the locations. They scout out good places to shoot and work with the director

and producers to decide which ones to use. They deal with authorities, property owners, etc., to get all the necessary permits and secure the location. From paying the big bucks to landlords to dealing with the public to keeping the locations clean, LMs have huge and varied jobs and usually require a lot of assistance with big productions. An LM may be redundant for us little guys because you only use one location, and it's your parents' basement. Or you may be "guerrilla" shooting anywhere you can set up your camera before someone kicks you out. Whatever the case, ensure your creative team thoroughly and realistically assesses the production needs concerning locations.

Art Director
Also known as the Production Designer, the Art Director decides what everything in the movie will look like, including the decorations on the walls of the main character's house, the design of special props, artistic themes, and colors in the costumes and environment where the scenes are taking place, the look of animations and special effects, etc. He or she also works with the Set Designer and builders to create artificial sets that specifically suit the artistic and technical needs of the production.

On a smaller project, you may or may not be building sets, or your Art Director may also be your Set Decorator and/or Props Master. This area depends on how much money you're spending and how elaborate the environment in which your story takes place is. Again, thoroughly assess your needs and balance them out with your budget. I recommend assigning at least one person to do this work, even on a tiny set.

Wardrobe, Hair and Make-Up
These are pretty self-explanatory; I won't go into detailed job descriptions. I will say that every one of these jobs is extremely important. You might have one

person doing all of them, but someone must.

Caterer and Craft Service

These may be the most important and loved people on your set, especially when you have a crew working for free. The crew's productivity will quickly go down the toilet if you don't feed them. This area is easily overlooked or underestimated. Again, a happy, effective crew is one whose stomach is full. The Caterer cooks the meals; Craft Services provides the snacks, drinks, and, most importantly, coffee. The Craft Service provider usually has a second job as the First Aid attendant. Having someone on your set who is well-versed in first aid is essential. The safety of your crew is even more important than their hunger. You may have one person doing these jobs, but have someone doing it. And provide nutritious, tasty, and energizing food that fits your budget. Trust me, you'll thank me later.

An electrician person who sets and adjusts the lights

Gaffer The Gaffer is the lighting director, who works with the Director of Photography to set lights for the shot.

Grip Grips are crew members who set objects that "control" the way light is cast on the set, move heavy objects, set up scaffolding, etc.

Key Grip: The head grip.

Dolly: A cart with wheels on which the camera is mounted for moving shots, controlled by the Dolly Grip, of course.

Dolly Grip: The Grip is in charge of pulling the dolly for moving shots.

Wheelchair Dolly: a staple of and credited to Robert Rodriguez and his first few independent films, in which he used an actual wheelchair for his dolly since he couldn't afford a real dolly.

Best Boy Assistant to the Gaffer or Key Grip. I have worked with Best Girls, too, BTW... (note: a department head's assistant is called a "best boy," "second," or "assistant," depending on the department)

First Assistant Director, also known as 1st A.D. is the traffic cop on set. This person keeps the set quiet, relays instructions via walkie-talkie to those off-set about what to prep, etc., and schedules the show, which may involve 150 scenes, dozens of actors and locations, conflicting schedules, changes in weather, etc.

Foley: credited to the inventor who designed sound effects recording for radio, filmmaker adopted this process (see any "Three Stooges" films). Aka: Film Sound Effects.

Second A.D. The 1st A.D.'s assistant helps manage the set, does paperwork, and supervises getting actors through make-up and wardrobe.

2nd 2nd A.D. Assistant to the Second A.D. In England, it is known as the 3rd A.D., which is probably less confusing unless you're a 2nd 2nd.

P.A. Production Assistant. These young men and women used to be called "gophers." They run errands, get coffee, clean up, move things, and try to keep everything quiet while the camera is rolling.

Script Supervisor: Usually a woman; old movie credits often listed them as "Script Girls." They are in charge of continuity (what line did the actor enter on, which hand did he pick up the glass with), making sure camera angles match, and keeping track of how much of the script has been shot.

Line Producer responsible for controlling the expenses and keeping costs down

The Loader Loads film into the camera and then unloads it for processing, usually in a small darkroom in the camera truck.

The Editor is responsible for assembling the film's parts into a coherent whole after it has been shot.

ADR Either Additional Dialogue Recording or Automated Dialogue Replacement, aka "looping"-- whatever the name, is the re-recording of dialogue due to background noise, a flubbed take, re-written dialogue, etc.
(Hint: if a film uses a voice-over narrator *too much*, usually it is because the film didn't make sense when they started editing it)

Second Unit: A small, usually rogue crew that shoots the shots that the cast is not needed for or First Unit didn't get, such as stunts, sunsets, beauty shots, close-ups of ashtrays, car drive-bys (if you don't see the stars face as the car drives by, he was probably miles away on his yacht, and 2nd Unit got the shot with a photo
double)

Photo Double: Someone dressed/made up to look like

an actor when the actor isn't there, usually for long shots, shots of hands, etc.

Production Designer See Art Director.

Stand-In People who resemble the stars of a film (in height and coloring) and "stand in" for an actor while the set is being lit and cameras are placed. Lighting can take a long time; the stand-ins get to sit under the hot lights while the set is being readied (which can take hours!) so the actors are fresh when the shot is good to go.

Locations If you are not on a soundstage, you are on one of these: any house, road, or building in the real world when invaded by a film crew. The Locations Department manages these, serving as a buffer between the needs of the film crew and reality (i.e., a rock and a hard place).

Location Scout person who searches out locations and photographs them to show the director, designer, and producer

Transportation is Responsible for everything involving vehicles. This includes maintenance and parking for trucks, trailers, cars, and vans.

I.A.T.S.E. is the union that represents much of the movie crew, including grips, projectionists, and wardrobe employees

Screen Actor's Guild (S.A.G): the union that represents the actors. SAG sets pay minimums for union members. Visit www.sag.org for membership requirements.

Stunt Coordinator: hires stunt people, plans and manages stunts, and ensures they are carried out safely

Principal Photography: the filming of all the speaking parts of the film, usually involving the major characters

Post-production is the process of completing the film. Involved in editing, adding music and sound effects, and preparing the film for release or distribution

Unit Manager/Unit Production Manager (UPM): Coordinates and manages the shooting schedules and locations and assists with the day-to-day financial operation of the shoot

A publicist is the person responsible for handling all media requests during filming. Also responsible for setting up interviews, managing press conferences, and arranging set visits.

Props: objects appearing on the set that are movable, including things like chairs, lamps, dishes, weapons

Set dressers find and place movable items (props) on the set, such as furniture, decorative pieces, posters, wall hangings, rugs, etc.

MOS When a scene is recorded without sound. The term is a somewhat playful reference to the German director Josef Von Sternberg, an acronym for "Mit Out Sound."

C47 Grip-speak for a clothespin.

Honey Wagon: A trailer with dressing rooms and toilet facilities for location shoots.

Craft Service The snack table on set has munchies,

cold drinks, coffee, etc. It is always a good place to look for AWOL crew members.

Caterer: The person responsible for bringing in full-scale dinners and lunches for the entire crew. Usually, Caterers on location shoots are nearby restaurants that provide food services to the film crew. Caterers and Craft Services are not the same.

Cyc Wall: A cyclorama (cyc) wall is commonly used as a green screen in film. A cyc is also a stage that has visibly seamless transitional curves between the floor and wall, as well as between the different walls on a multi-wall cyc stage. With proper lighting, it gives the appearance of an endless or horizon-less background. It is commonly seen in advertisements and music videos.

Some soundstages keep their cyc walls painted white when not in use, and the product that uses them can paint them blue or green as needed. Instead of having a corner at the bottom, the cyc wall is curved, so there are fewer shadows when the green (or blue) is replaced in editing.

People use the term "cyc" simply because that's faster and easier to spell or say than cyclorama.

Breakfast Burritos are a Wonderful breakfast tradition on set. Scrambled eggs and whatever else you want are wrapped in a burrito. Naturally insulated and fairly drip-proof, they're perfect for those on the go at 6:00 AM.

Sides ¼-size copies of the script pages to be shot that day; handed out to the cast and crew in the morning. Small enough to go in one's pocket.

Taco Cart: Any rolling cart containing props, sound equipment, grip gear, etc.

Abbey Singer: Second-to-last-shot of the night. Named after the infamous production crew person who often called "Last Shot" prematurely. Thus, the second to last shot is the "Abby Singer" because it is not the last shot.

Martini Shot: The Last shot of the night. On most production sets, this shot has a bad habit of turning into the Abbey Singer, meaning the director will call for yet another shot after this Martini Shot has been called, effectively making it the "Abbey Singer" shot.

Wrap: That's the end.

www.ingramcontent.com/pod-product-compliance
Lightning Source LLC
Chambersburg PA
CBHW072018230526
45479CB00008B/289